When Angels Gather Here

By Susan M. Geiger

When Angels Gather Here by Susan M. Geiger

ISBN13: 978-1-59755-261-5

Published by: ADVANTAGE BOOKS™
www.advbookstore.com

Library of Congress Control Number: 2011936332

Drawings by Susan Geiger and Students

First Printing: November 2011
11 12 13 14 15 16 17   10 9 8 7 6 5 4 3 2 1
Printed in the United States of America

Dedicated in Loving Memory to my husband
Nicholas Taliaferro
who always believed that
"Love alone creates."

Introduction

"When Angels Gather Here" was written about teaching experiences with the Parks and Recreation Departments of the City of Palmdale and Los Angeles County, and also from private instruction. The lessons were created from eight-week sessions or from classes that continued month-to-month. The ten lessons in this book are meant as a guide to basic drawing techniques, coupled with an emphasis on freedom of expression.

The lessons are the result of seven years of experimentation and dialogue with students aged seven to sixteen. The classes were serious and fun, with hard work as a motto. The children were eager to learn about beauty, and I tried to convey my understanding of art in a manner that was original and challenging. They responded in important and unique ways that kept us all enthralled. We always had a good time.

Hopefully, these lessons will continue to help children to understand art and learn to realize their special worth by what they create. This has been my ideal. I wish you great success.

Susan Geiger
Ojai, California
May, 2011

Table Of Contents

Lesson One, Part One

Contour Drawing of Hand positions to Form Tree Shape

Explain to students that we don't use erasers for the first and second lessons. Next, very important, tell them that it is the <u>experience</u> of drawing, not the result, that we are after. With a well sharpened 2B drawing pencil, open sketchbook to fresh page. Instruct children to begin on the lower part of the page. This would be near the middle where the trunk of the tree should start. Now, mention that you may not look down at the paper while you are drawing your hand.

Show example of contour drawing of hand. Read "Art notes." Tell students to try to make hand positions conform to tree trunk and branch shapes. You will be building your hand shapes on top of each other. When you begin, remember you will be concentrating very hard. Once you put your pencil point down on the paper, you can't look at your drawing until you have finished.

Pretend that you are touching the skin of your hand with the pencil point. Go as slowly as you can to catch details, noticing wrinkles, nails and creases. Outline the hand first. If you want to put in nails and lines, do that later. Perhaps your hand will look strange, that means you are doing it right. Remember, in this exercise we are not concerned with the result. If drawing looks odd, you've got the right idea. You will need at least four or five hand shapes to finish the tree.

Make sure you put hand in different positions, and remember to pretend that you are touching the skin of the hand with the pencil point while you are drawing it. This is very important. Also, try not to draw the hand shapes too small (show example). Now before beginning, loosen up the fingers, stretch them to the ceiling, and take three deep breaths. Remember to concentrate on the experience of drawing, of making a line.

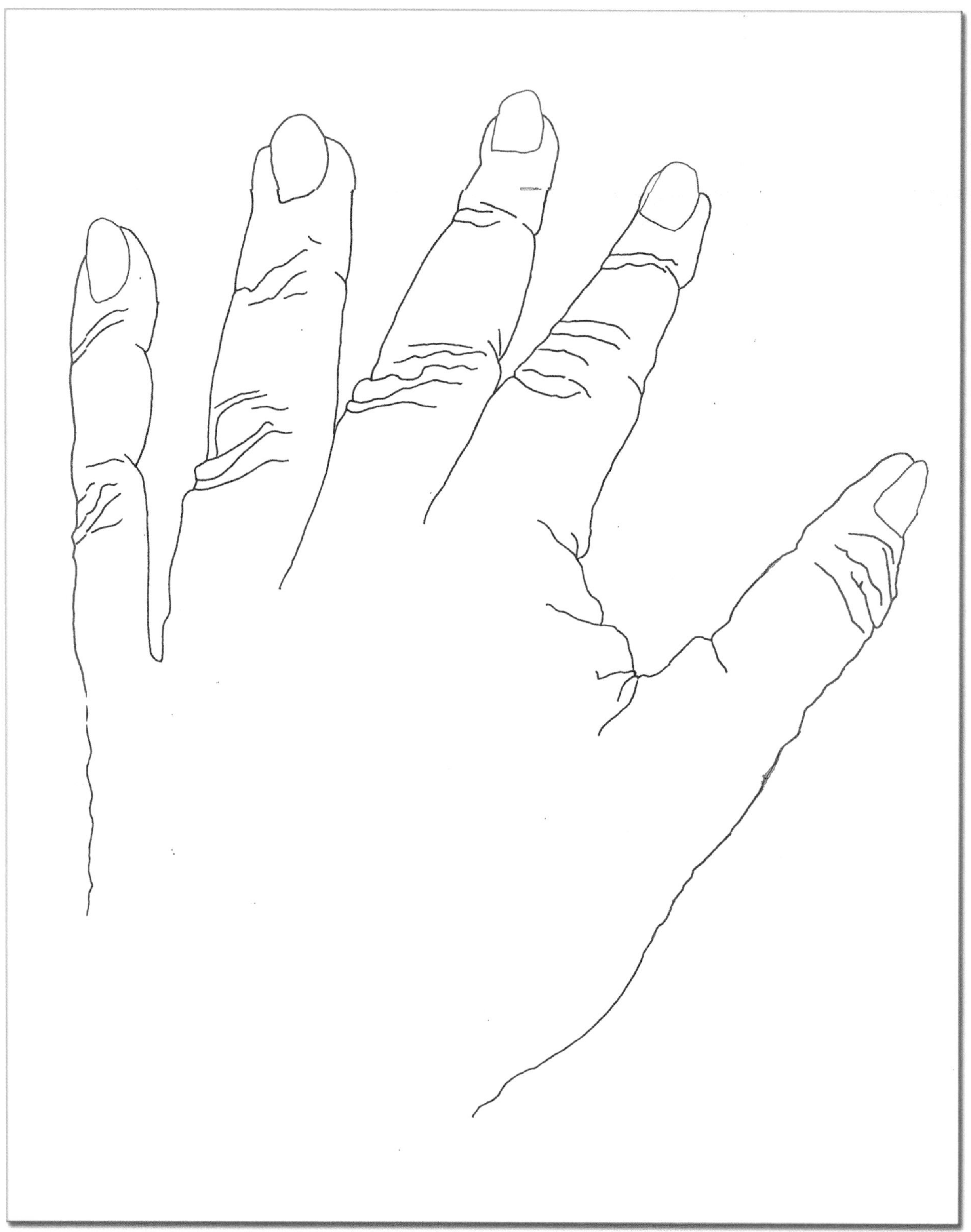

Illustration 1

Lesson One, Part Two

Color Theory Using Complementary Colors

Have a color wheel handy. Most students have probably made one in earlier years. Pass out six pieces of 8 ½" x 11" construction paper, scissors, and glue sticks. The colors should be basic. I stay away from pastel colors. Try red, orange, blue, green, yellow, and pink or violet. Also, after explaining lesson and showing examples, pass out to each student both a black and white or manila piece of paper. One is for background. They can choose either; the other is for a glue worksheet. The children can do their gluing on the paper so it doesn't get on the table.

Now, let's begin by explaining that color theory is a science. You can make your colors bright or subdued by what you place next to each color. The complementary colors are opposite each other on the color wheel. The opposite of blue is orange, the opposite of red is green, and the opposite of yellow is purple or violet. What I like to say is that when I want my color to be as strong as it can be, I put its complementary color near it or on it. If I want my blue to be vibrant, I put orange next to it or somewhere on the paper. The same idea works with red and green, and yellow and violet. (Mention the Impressionist painter, Seurat, and how he created a vibration of color by using complementary colors next to each other. He called this "illumination."

Have the children make shapes with the six different colors of construction paper, avoiding black and white. They can cut or tear shapes. I fold a piece of paper in half and cut or tear symmetrical designs. It is best to have different sized shapes; large, medium and small, for composition's sake. What I ask is for the students to make a "bank" of colors, so they will be making design decisions. A "bank" can be 10-15 or so different shapes in the six colors. The children can put the bank of material above their background paper so it is easily within reach.

<u>Example</u>: Put a scrap of green on red, and the same size scrap of green on yellow. The colors should look different even though the green paper is the same. The

complementary color will appear brighter while the green on yellow will appear more blue. Because green is a combination of yellow and blue, the yellow background is bleeding the yellow color out of the green, making it blue-green. This is how color theory works.

Next, use glue sticks to paste down shapes, making sure the edges are glued down and not curling. Paste down all six colors, using each color at least once, keeping in mind complementary theme.

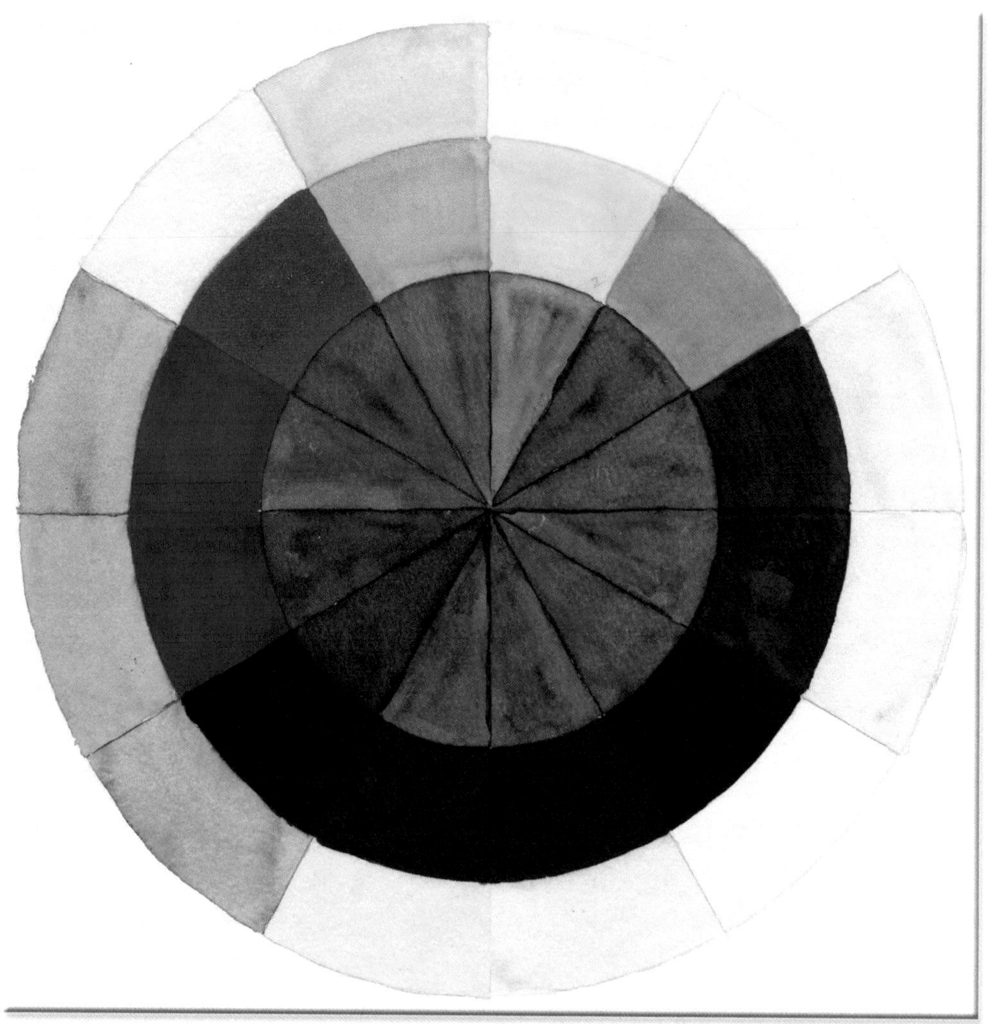

Illustration 2

Illustration 3

Illustration 4

Lesson One, Part Three

Coloring Tree Shape of Hands

I think it is best to let the students choose between colored pencils or oil pastels. The pastels are more vibrant, but messy and hard-won detail can be lost.

Ask the children to use what they learned from the color theory lesson in their drawing. Give a brief demonstration of shading and blending. With shading, make a series of light strokes in a small rectangle or square, about 1-inch square. I use a light stroke which I call "feathering." First sketch vertical lines close together, then horizontal, then diagonal in both directions. Demonstrate technique.

This shading technique is just like cross-hatching but done with colored pencil. Later on, we shade with graphite using the same idea. Try to get a soft tone, not scratchy or scribbly. This is a time-consuming lesson, so if the class is almost finished, the children can do it at home.

Blending colors is making overlays to get another color; try laying green on top of yellow for a spring green, etc. It is a kind of self-taught experiment. The children like it.

Now, just turn the kids loose and let them color their trees. Some students like to stick to realistic color patterns; others really go wild. It might be good to show some work of the Fauves to them. I really feel it is good to try and free up the children, and let them experience inspiration and decision-making.

Illiustration 5

Lesson Two

Contour and Cross-Contour Drawing of Driftwood

For this lesson, use pencil, pen and ink, and charcoal.

Collect small pieces of driftwood in interesting, pleasing shapes, 12″ to 16″ or in length. In the desert I found my samples at a yard sale. Have about eight on hand to choose from, depending on the size of your class. I use an old ammunition box with a top for storage, and then bring it to class and let the children pick out pieces that they like.

Begin by having each child choose a piece of driftwood and place it in front of the sketchpad, or whatever is most helpful. Go over the rules of contour drawing. Remember not to look down at the paper while drawing; pretend that you are touching the wood with your pencil point, and do not work too small. Sharpen a 2B drawing pencil to a fine point and start. It is better to begin in the middle of the page with the sketch pad in a horizontal position.

After the contour drawing is completed, point out that there are curly lines and creases on the inside of the driftwood. To draw these inside your contour drawing is called "cross-contour." Pick a starting point, and without looking down, concentrate on the inner lines; they may be difficult to follow. Again, don't worry if you draw outside your original form. Remember, a good contour drawing looks unusual.

After the children have finished their first drawing, let them trade for a new driftwood. Then take a break. Make sure that students are not working too small.

Using a bamboo ink stick (pen) and a jar of black drawing ink (small Higgins bottles), take out manila paper or newsprint 18″ x 24″ or 24″ x 30.″ Instruct students <u>not</u> to leave the pen in the ink jar when they are not using it, as it is too easy to tip over the ink bottle. The ink pen has a small hole in the nib. Notice that you want to cover the hole with ink when you dip the pen-point into the ink. Next, touch the pen nib to the inner side of the jar to knock off the blob of ink resting on the pen point. This will help to keep the drawing neat.

Demonstrate first how to use the bamboo pen, making lines and shapes. If the ink runs out, repeat introductory instructions. Show the children how to hold the pen, as if it were a pencil, so they are looking down over the point of the pen. If the ink is gone, do not scratch or scribble, as this dulls the nib. Always make sure there is ink in the pen before you draw.

With the same piece of driftwood (I think it might be easier since the students are familiar with its shape), try a contour and cross-contour drawing with pen and ink on newsprint. The line work is exciting and sometimes the ink puddles a little when you start a new line. Of course, now you have a chance to look down at your drawing because ink may run out. It will be fun to learn to look and draw at the same time.

If time permits, bring a few broken charcoal pieces and let the children experiment using either the point or side of the stick. They can shade their ink drawings or start a new one. Art chamois' are great for technique. The students will use them in the portrait lesson. They can smooth over the charcoal by rubbing the chamois on it; the shading will lighten. It is good to end this lesson with experimentation while the children are warmed up, and this will also loosen them up. Freedom of expression is one of our goals.

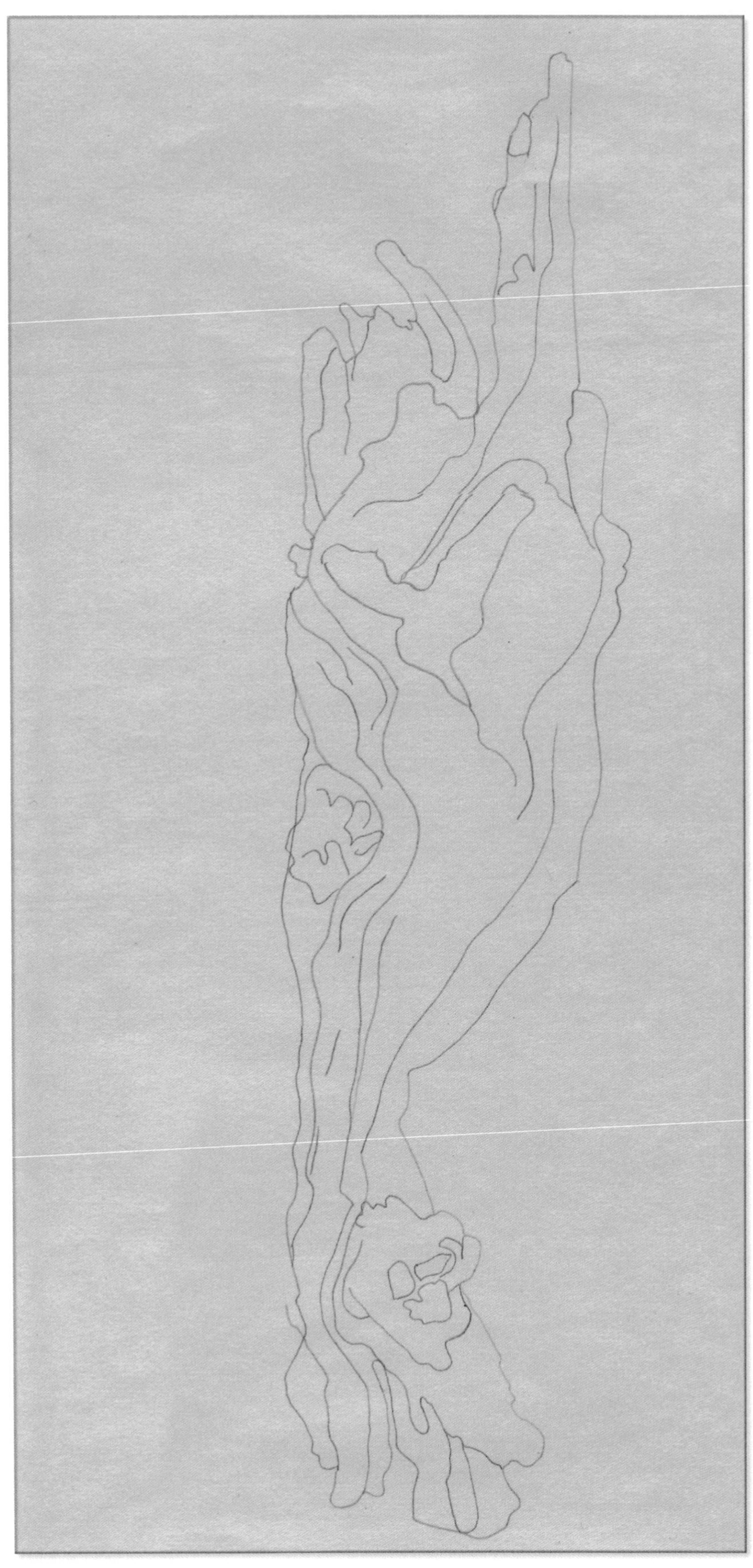

Illustration 6

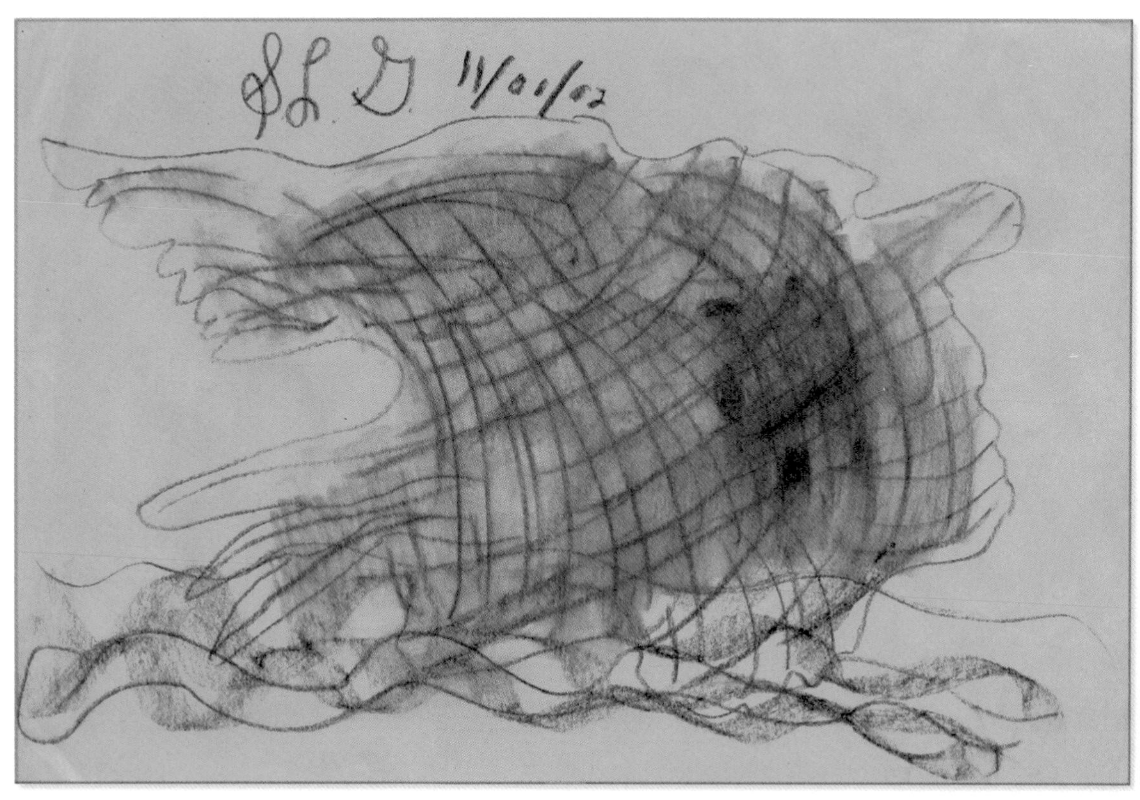

Illustration 7

Lesson Three, Part One

Point-to-Point Drawing

Use a knobby branch as an art subject, with one for each child, preferably without foliage, e.g. a winter or early spring branch with buds.

Children may now use erasers. Explain: "If you do not like the line you have drawn, erase it." Put drawing pads in a vertical position. You may desire to lay the branch beside the sketch book or prop it up in a weighted jar, so the subject is standing up; this seems best.

To begin, let the students know that they may now look down at the paper. First, find a starting point near the bottom of the branch. Next, locate a good stopping point farther up the branch, probably at a joint, nub or knob. Place your pencil down at the paper (bottom of page), looking at your first point. Then draw without looking down, to stop-point.

You may now use an eraser, but try not to use it too often. Follow this procedure, drawing from point-to-point until finished. It is a bit like contour drawing with more freedom. Remember to pick a new point as your drawing progresses and follow through. Also, this is a very nice lesson to ink. Your lines will be different lengths according to your start and stop points. Don't make this too difficult; find easy stopping points.

Lesson Three, Part Two

Negative Space Drawing

Subject matter I have used: Plant foliage, antique wire lantern, old plough bridle, bones with holes.

Start with a card table set in middle of art tables. Put some pretty fabric down or just a sheet, and arrange objects so you can see through to another object. The idea is to create exciting space around and between the setup. Leaves on plants and branches sometimes are all you would need.

Begin by saying that this is a very <u>relaxing</u> way to draw. We will <u>not</u> be drawing the object (positive space), but the space around and through it (negative space). A line is formed, we notice, where the space meets the object. We will only be drawing the space next to the object, around it and perhaps holes. Try to use your contour drawing experience. Concentrate on the space. You will find a drawing developing full of design elements. Have fun picking shapes made by the space. This is a good way to learn to look. Let your eyes and hands enjoy this different way of drawing and seeing.

Illustration 8

Lesson Four

Contrast: Darks and Lights in Composition

This is a lesson that I created on the spot in class. You will need black and white construction paper and glue sticks, with manila or white as background. Stark contrast photographs are necessary. I have used bright sunlight and shadow with wildflowers, as well as a snowfall and trees. This is a popular lesson, and very instructional.

First, explain about scale and proportion (what is one-third up on the side of the photograph will be one-third up on the construction paper). Next, map out the drawing, using the dark areas in the photo. Inform the children that if they are sketching or painting outside in nature, they should look for areas in the composition in terms of darks and lights. This concept is also employed in Lesson Five on Portraits.

Begin by tearing pieces of black construction paper to build up the dark areas you see in the photograph. The pieces should be fairly small. Using glue sticks, create the dark forms on white background. Try to match areas as accurately as possible but leave room for experimentation. In other words, don't be too tight about your shapes. Just try to get it right. The design can be very appealing. Remember your dark shapes are growing; you are building the dark areas with your scraps.

The same composition, or another one, can be made using complementary colors. For example, for your darks use blue, for your lights use orange, or use orange as a background color. This is a good composition exercise and also teaches design. The students will learn to look and learn scale while creating. When gluing, make sure that edges don't curl up. Keep it neat and work slowly. This is a good way to "listen" to your drawing as you make it.

Illustration 9

Lesson Five

Portrait

Have available:

- Charcoal paper 11" x 17" (Strathmore makes pads)
- Pressed charcoal sticks
- Art chamois
- Kneaded erasers
- Colored pastel chalks
- Krylon workable fixative

Show an example. (Illustration 11) I did this exercise with oil pastels just so the idea of "freedom" of expression is emphasized.

- Draw a large egg shape with charcoal to fill paper.
- Using construction lines, draw a horizontal line halfway through egg shape.
- Divide lower half into thirds. Make two points and draw horizontal lines through points from side to side.
- Finally, draw centerline from top to bottom through middle part of egg shape.

Eyes

On middle horizontal line (this would be your first line), make two equidistant points on either side of Center Line. Then make two more points for end of eye.

Explain that eyes are generally almond shaped. With line half above and half below construction line, connect with points, drawing curved line, make eye shape.

Nose

On next horizontal line , draw semi-circle beneath line on either side of the Center Line. Then draw small semi-circles for nostrils on either side of the Center Line beginning at line. Next, draw nose symmetrically to extend into eyebrows.

Mouth

On last horizontal line at Center Line, make small V-Shape for beginning of lips. On line, draw equidistant points for end of mouth. Curve from V-mark to points. Below construction line, draw a large semi-circle for bottom of lips. For parting lips, follow V-Shape, curve slightly and connect to endpoints.

Ears and Hair

Ears are between eyebrows and end of nose. For hair, use side (if you like) of charcoal stick and sketch in bangs, parts, long hair or short hair.

Finishing

Pick a light and a dark colored pastel, and sketch in light and dark areas of the face. Next, draw eyeballs and have fun blending with the chamois. Put a small neck below on either side of the Center Line. Shade.

When you are finished, spray with fixative in a well-ventilated area.

Have students pick a partner and let them draw each other.

Illustration 10

Illustration 11

Illustration 12

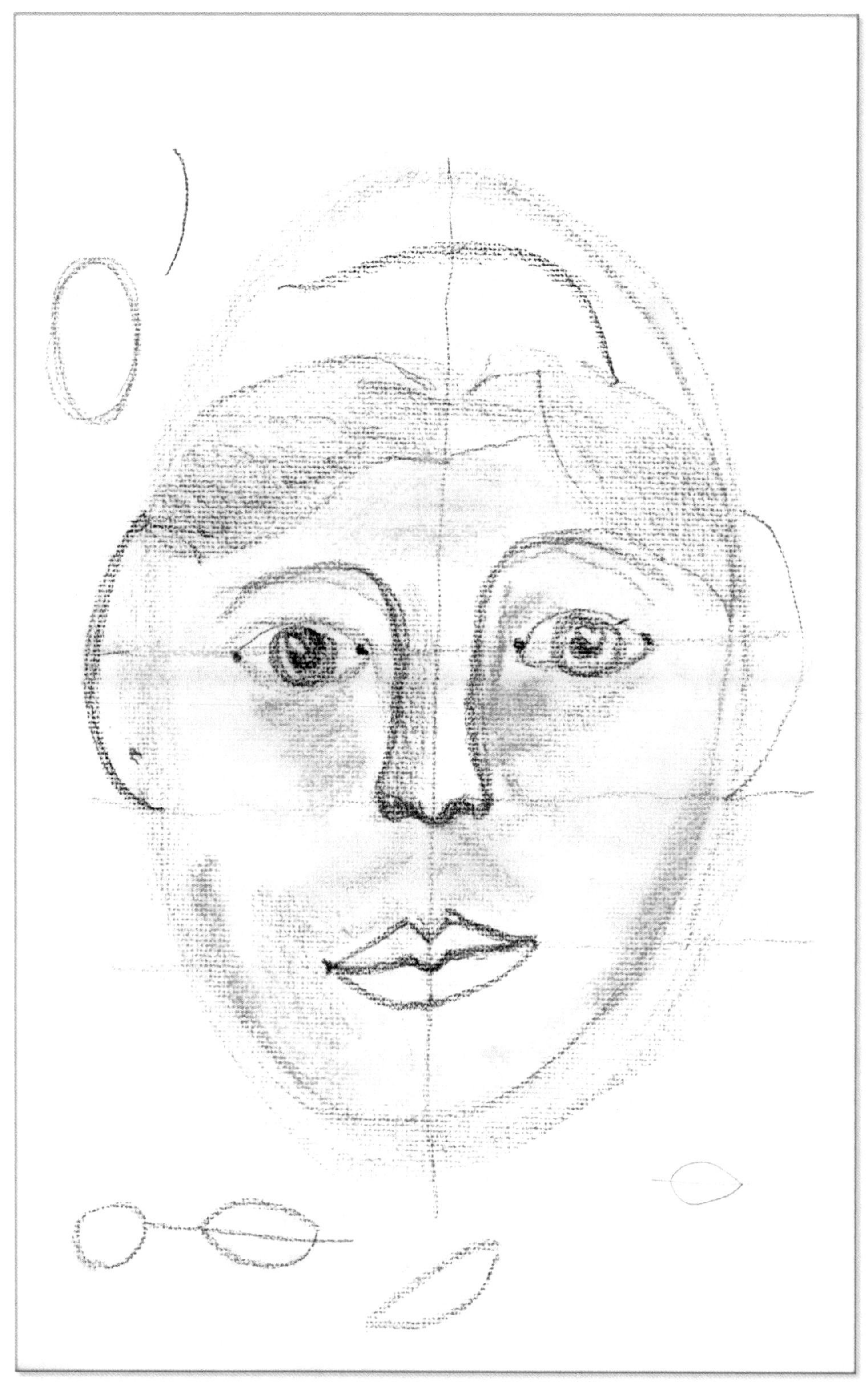

Illustration 13

Lesson Six

Still-Life

Using a card table with drawing tables or easels around it in a "U" shape, create a set-up with fabric and objects. I found things in the desert antique shops such as: old leather plough bridle, lantern, driftwood, cow skull bones, large crude basket, and some African fabric. Arrange so your still-life can be viewed from all angles.

Have children draw "thumb-nail" sketches in their pads. Draw three horizontal and vertical blocks on the page, 3" x 4." Find pleasing compositions, taking into account all four sides of the block. You may use a small mat to find or make compositions. Choose the one you like best and enlarge on your drawing pad.

Draw composition for about twenty minutes. Use what you learned about scale. If sketch starts one-third up block, then drawing will begin one-third up page, etc. Use techniques previously learned: contour, cross-contour, point-to-point, and negative space. If you want to shade, go back to colored pencil technique and try your HB pencil. The lead is harder and lends itself to lighter shading than the 2B. Remember dark and light areas.

Most importantly, look and draw at the same time. You can find clues in composition to help with your drawing line. Look for reference points to create. For example, where is the bone in relation to the basket or lantern? Foreground is lower on the page. If an object is in front of another object, notice that the first object is lower in your composition. Background will be higher on the page. Look for relationships between your subject matter. It is like charting a map. Does the top of one part meet the middle of something else? These are drawing relationships.

When children have used up the space in their composition, have them notice darks and lights. Shade, using the feathering cross-hatching technique. Imagine that you are really painting in black and white. Use the HB pencil for lighter areas and your softer 2B for the dark areas. This will teach a little bit about the difference in leads. Most of all, try to tell a story with your picture. You always have "something to say" when you create a visual piece of language.

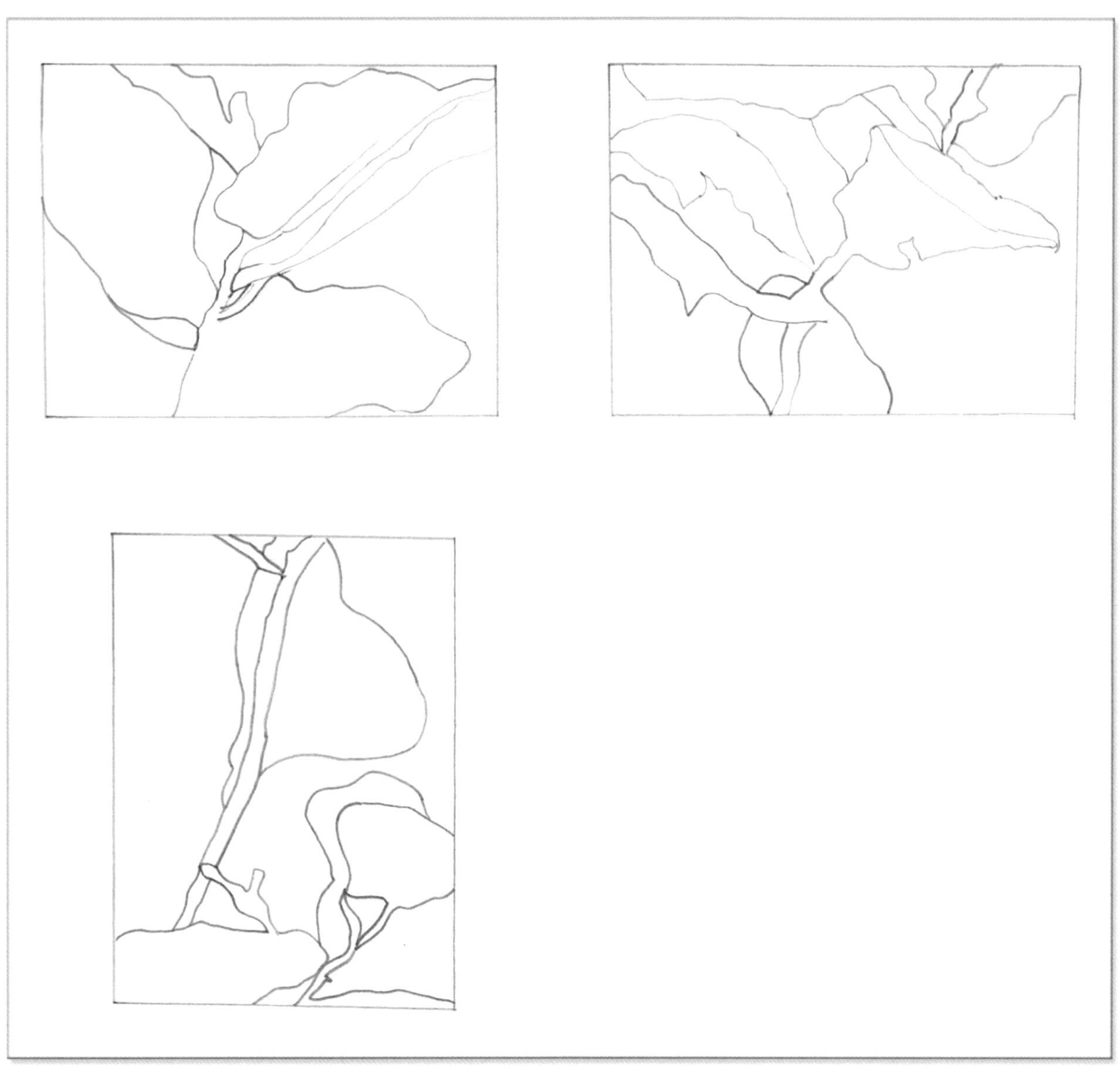

Illustration 14

Lesson Seven

Value Scale and Shading with Light Source

Part 1: Value Scale

On your drawing pad, on a new sheet of paper, draw a long, thin, rectangular block. It should be 8 inches long and 1-inch high. Using a ruler, divide into eight one-inch sections.

In your first block, beginning at the left side, using shading technique, make your darkest dark. Then, gradually proceeding to the right, make each square lighter until your last square is the lightest light. This is a difficult lesson. What you are creating is called a value scale.

Part 2: Shading with Light Source

Show examples of shading with Light Source. Airbrush examples are included on shading with light source of cube, circle, cylinder and cone.

Have children draw a 3-dimensional cube, cylinder, cone and circle and shade accordingly. This part of the lesson is almost mathematical and is very popular, but requires attention from the teacher.

If time permits, tear pieces of construction paper in light, medium, and dark tones. Glue down colors with glue stick, pasting on drawn objects like ball, vase, glass, box shape to establish light source. Examples of colors to use could be yellow, orange and red. The finished piece resembles a mosaic with yellow as a light source.

Illustration 15

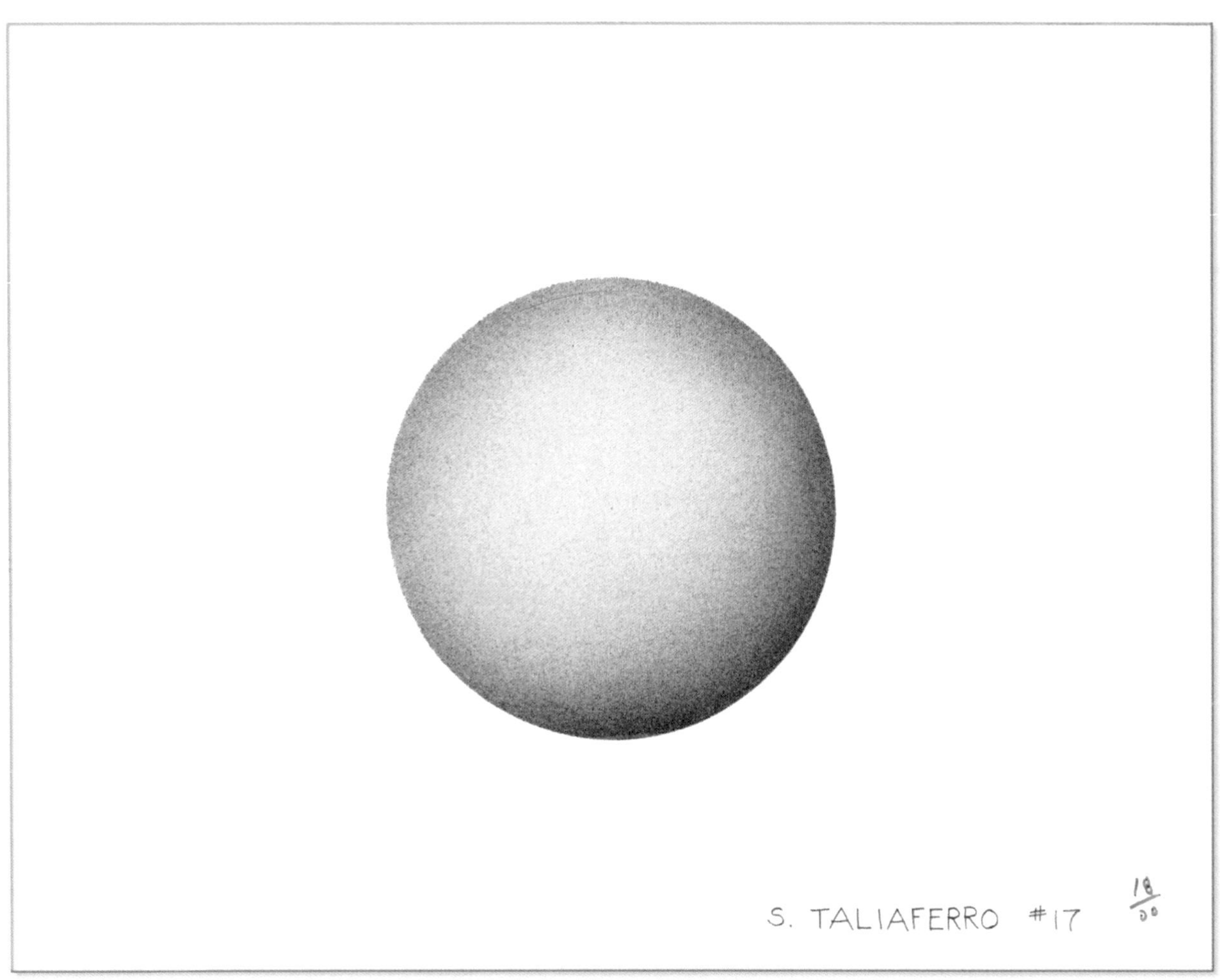

Illustration 16

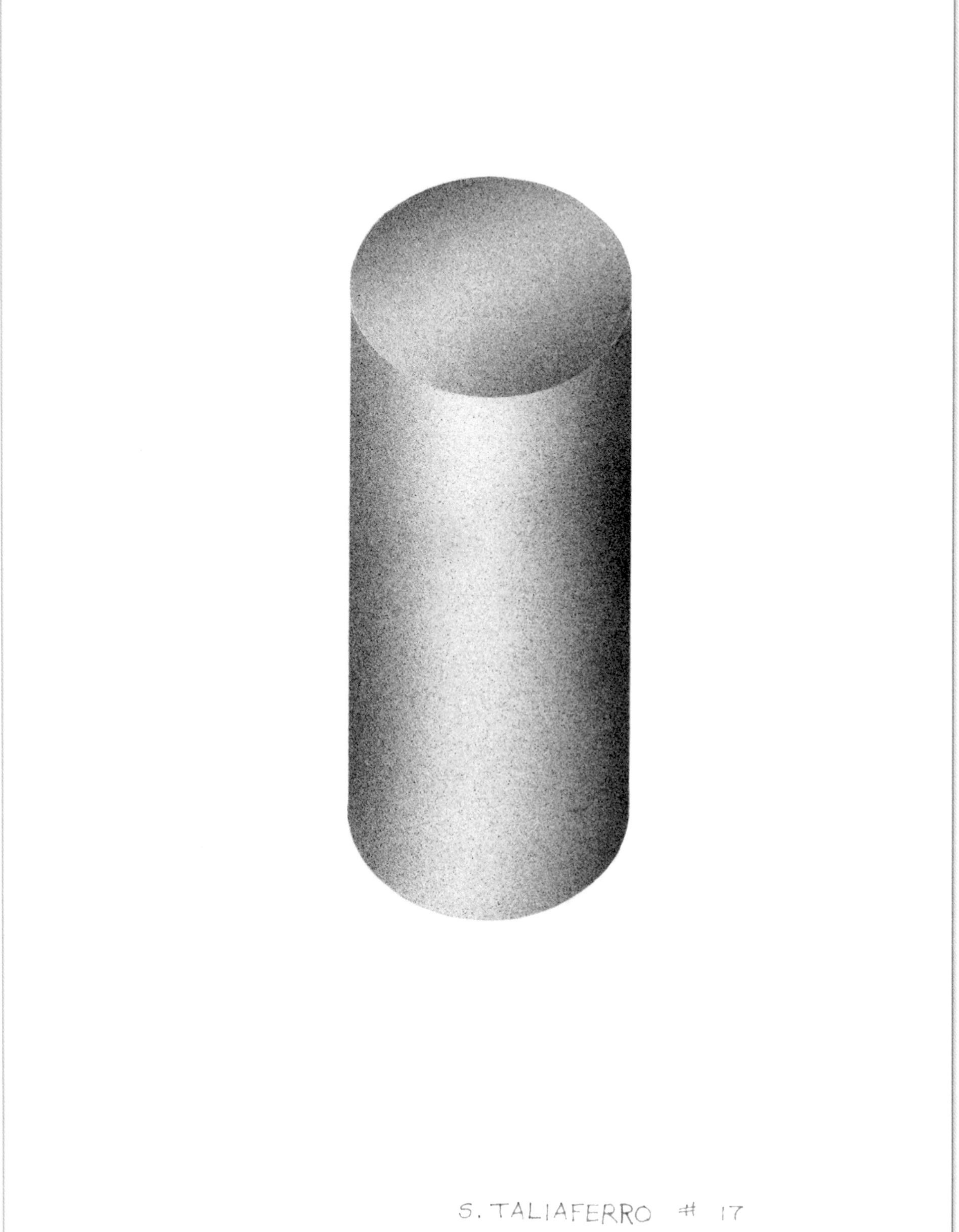

Illustration 17

Illustration 18

Illustration 19

Illustration 20

Lesson Eight

Symmetry

Explain the concept of symmetry by showing how the human body is a good example. If you draw a center line from head to toe, everything is equidistant: eyes, ears, nose, breast, arms, etc. Return to portrait lesson to point out how the center line determines where the drawing points go, remembering eyes, nose, mouth, neck. We use reference points when drawing symmetrically.

Using clay vases, bottles, and anything that will work, teach by plotting points equidistant from the center line. First, pick an object and draw in center line. Then draw horizontal lines through base, widest point, narrowest point, and top. Plot points by eye on either side of center line, making points are the same distance on either side of center line. Remember base (bottom) is not flat, but an ellipse. After your points are complete, draw curves through points for the form. The top, or lip, is also an ellipse.

It is best to use a harder lead to sketch in the object lightly, and then go over curves with a softer, darker lead. Draw once before creating composition. The artist Morandi has many jar and bottle paintings and etchings. These are good examples.

Using bottles, vases, jars, etc., create set-up on white fabric. Have light source available. Preliminary sketches may be helpful. Create composition, stressing background and foreground. Mention again that foreground is always lower on the page. Remember to look for clues from objects (relationships) while drawing. Overhead lighting is not too helpful; window or spot lighting is better. Shade as desired. Different colored jars and bottles are important to balance composition, as well as lines and forms. Try to harmonize; creating a drawing that is pleasing to the eyes. You may want to incorporate shadows too, as part of the whole drawing.

One last thought: line weight makes a nice drawing. If you bear down with the pencil to get a heavy, thick line; try lightening up and get a thinner, lighter line. This use of weight can make a beautiful difference in your drawing. Be sensitive. Talk to your drawing with your pencil and it will talk back and give you ideas. This is called dialogue and is an important part of creating something you and others will like.

Illustration 21

Lesson Nine

Collage

Using calendars, magazines, old unsuccessful work, wrapping paper, recycled construction paper – tear or cut, using a theme. This could be written on board. A weekly calendar with inspirational quotes works well. Let the children pick out one or two, then create an "image bank" of pictures that go with the meaning or message.

Work on large paper. Without leaving too much white background, create a collage. Place pictures in front of you in a pile, then begin to build. I call this "painting with pictures." Stress textures, color theory, shapes and sizes. Try to keep one idea.

Decision – making.

Lesson Ten

Clay and Plaster Sculpture

With cutting wire, give each child about a 6″ x 8″ block of clay. Using thumbs, make a well, leaving 1 ½″ all around. Smooth bottom and inner walls.

Using objects (tools, jewelry, shells, plastic animals, doll heads, toys) press into clay and remove, leaving imprint (negative image).
Press into bottom and inner sides.

Mix Plaster of Paris into liquid consistency of heavy cream.

Pour Plaster of Paris into clay well to top and let set.

When almost hard, insert horseshoe nail into plaster (where you want to hang the sculpture). When plaster is hot to touch, it has set.
Carefully peel away clay from plaster cast.

Earthenware clay leaves a pink hue. Gray Stoneware is better color wise. You can wash if messy.

Paint with watercolors and seal with glossy fixative.

This is a good exercise in positive and negative: what was pushed in – now stands out.

List Of Materials

Spiral-bound good quality Drawing Pad, at least 14″ x 17″ – Canson
Newsprint Paper 18″ x 24″ or 24″ x″30
Charcoal Pad 11″ x 17″ – Strathmore
Drawing Pencils 2 each: 2B,HB – Eagle Turquoise
Pink Pearl Eraser (large)
Colored Pencils, beginning artist quality, minimum set of 12
Oil Pastels, set of 24, inexpensive beginning artist
Pressed charcoal sticks
Kneaded eraser
Chamois
Chalk Pastels to share – Grumbacher (1 set)
Bamboo Pen and Drawing Ink (black)

Final Project (Lesson 10):
Water Colors, student quality: cadmium red, yellow, cobalt blue
Small and medium inexpensive water-color brushes
Plastic palette or pie plates
Plaster of Paris & plastic bucket for mixing
Clay (from a college bookstore) not modeling clay
Acrylic clear glossy sealant spray, from a craft store

Have available:
Glue sticks
Electric Pencil Sharpener
Scissors
Construction paper
Krylon Workable Fixative
Small mats (available from student art supply catalog) square or rectangular 2″ inside cut

Art Notes

By me, to read while children are drawing

Art is nothing to be afraid of.

Every person loves beauty.

There are perfect compositions all around us.

Mistakes can be lessons learned.

Having good tools is important.

Being creative helps in making good art.

Art is a way of talking to oneself.

Other people can understand you through art.

Art is a visual language.

Drawing is like music or dance – it has rhythm.

Looking is a task, sometimes very hard, sometimes very easy.

You don't have to copy or duplicate.

Interpretation is what is important.

You'll be surprised at how art will happen.

Art is fun, sometimes hard or frustrating, but you have to follow it through

Having ideas is important.

You can always change it. Almost always.

Art takes time.

Art takes love and peace.

Art is sharing, that is half the fun.

Remember that nothing is small in the eyes of God.
Do all that you do with love.
ST. THERESE OF LISIEUX

Susan Geiger is available for speaking engagements and personal appearances. For more information contact:

Susan Geiger
C/O Advantage Books
PO Box 160847
Altamonte Springs, FL 32779
info@ advbooks.com

To purchase additional copies of this book online, go to:

www.WhenAngelsGatherHere.com

or call our toll free order line:

1-888-383-3110 (Book Orders Only)

Longwood, Florida, USA
"we bring dreams to life"™
www.advbooks.com